KENTUCKY

in words and pictures

BY DENNIS B. FRADIN

ILLUSTRATIONS BY RICHARD WAHL

MAPS BY LEN W. MEENTS

 CHILDRENS PRESS, CHICAGO

For Noah E. Bonham-Brindel

For their help, the author thanks:
Dr. Lathel Duffield, Director of the Museum of Anthropology, University of Kentucky
Linda Anderson, Assistant Librarian, Kentucky Historical Society

Cumberland Gap, Middlesboro, Kentucky

Library of Congress Cataloging in Publication Data

Fradin, Dennis B
  Kentucky in words and pictures.

  SUMMARY: Briefly introduces the history of the Bluegrass State and its geography, industries, cities, major tourist attractions, and famous citizens.
  1. Kentucky—Juvenile literature. [1. Kentucky]
1. Wahl, Richard, 1939-   II. Meents, Len W.
III. Title.
F451.3.F72   976.9   80-25810
ISBN 0-516-03917-2

Picture Acknowledgments:
KENTUCKY DEPARTMENT OF TOURISM, PHOTO SECTION—2, 10 (left), 16 (right), 17 (right), 20 (lower right), 27 (middle), 28 (left), 29 (right), 34 (2), 36 (left), 38
DEPARTMENT OF PUBLIC INFORMATION, MULTI MEDIA SERVICES—4, 7, 8, (left), 9, 10 (right), 16 (left), 17 (left), 20 (left), 23, 25, 26, 27 (far left & right),28 (middle & right), 29 (left & middle), 30 (left), 31 (2), 32, 33, 35
JAMES P. ROWAN—20 (top right), 24, 36 (right), 43
U.S. ARMY, FORT KNOX—30 (right)
MISSOURI HISTORICAL SOCIETY—8 (right)

Kentucky

The word *Kentucky* (ken • TUCK • ee) comes from an Indian word. People don't agree on what it means. Some say it means the *Land of Tomorrow*. Others think it means the *Dark and Bloody Ground*.

Kentucky is famous for the many horses that are raised in its "Bluegrass Region." The most famous horse race in the United States, the Kentucky Derby, is held in Louisville (LOO • ee • vill). But Kentucky has a lot more than horses! It is our number one coal-mining state. It is a leading state for growing tobacco.

Do you know where President Abraham Lincoln was born? Or where Jefferson Davis—the president of the Confederacy (con • FED • er • ah • see)—was born? Do you know where Daniel Boone built a town?

Big Bone Lick

You'll soon see that the answer to all these questions is: Kentucky, the Bluegrass State!

About 300 million years ago, much of Kentucky was covered by swamps. Plants lived in the swamps. The plants died. They formed a thick layer of plant material. Over long periods of time this hardened into coal.

In past ages, many unusual animals lived in Kentucky. Mastodons (MASS • tah • donz) and mammoths (MAM • uths) were there. They looked like big, hairy elephants. Giant beavers and wolves lived there, too. There is a place in Kentucky where the bones of many ancient animals have been found. It is called Big Bone Lick. Long ago, animals went there to eat salt. Some got stuck in the mud and died there.

Indians came to Kentucky at least 15,000 years ago. The earliest Indians moved from place to place as they hunted. It is thought that they hunted mammoths. Stone spearpoints and tools of the early people have been found.

By 1,000 years ago, Indians in Kentucky were farming. This was an important change. Farming meant that the Indians could stay in one place. Remains of their villages have been found.

The modern Indian tribes in Kentucky were related to the ancient people. The Shawnee (shaw • NEE), Chickasaw (CHICK • ah • saw), and Cherokee (CHAIR • uh • kee) were three of the tribes that lived and hunted in Kentucky.

The Indians built houses out of wood and bark. They hunted deer and other small game. They ate the meat. They used the skins to make clothes. The Indians caught catfish and turtles in Kentucky's many streams. They gathered wild fruits and nuts in the forests. They grew corn, squash, and beans for eating. The Indians also grew tobacco, which they smoked in clay pipes. Smoking was a big part of Indian ceremonies. They felt that the smoke carried their messages to the gods.

Raft on the Cumberland River

Nobody knows who first explored Kentucky. English and French explorers entered Kentucky in the late 1600s and early 1700s. But these first visits were short.

Dr. Thomas Walker was one of the first explorers to spend a lot of time in Kentucky. Walker led some men from Virginia in 1750. They made their way through a pass in the Appalachian (ap • uh • LATCH • ih • un) Mountains. Dr. Walker named this pass the "Cumberland Gap." Walker and his men then explored the mountains and rivers of eastern Kentucky.

Above: Buffalo still graze in Kentucky.
Right: Print taken from a 1819 portrait of Daniel Boone

In the 1760s men called "long hunters" came to
Kentucky. They were called that because they spent long
periods of time hunting in the wilderness. Daniel Boone
was the most famous long hunter who came to Kentucky.

Boone was born in Pennsylvania (pen • sill • VAIN • ee •
ah) in 1734. Indians taught him how to hunt and live in
the woods. Daniel Boone loved to hunt. He didn't like
places that were crowded. He always wanted plenty of
what he called "elbow room."

Daniel Boone was living in North Carolina when he heard about Kentucky. It was said to be filled with buffalo, wild turkeys, and deer. Boone hunted in Kentucky in 1767 and again in 1769. He fell in love with the place.

In 1773, Daniel Boone decided to bring his family to live in Kentucky. Other settlers came with them. Usually, Daniel Boone stayed out of the Indians' way or made friends with them. But this time Indians killed one of Daniel Boone's sons. The settlers had to turn back. The next year, in 1774, a man named James Harrod (HAIR • od) founded Kentucky's first non-Indian town. It was called Harrodsburg.

Left: Portrait of James Harrod
Below: Fort Harrod in Harrodsburg

Fort Boonesborough has been reconstructed as part of a state park.

In 1775, the Transylvania (tranz • ill • VAIN • ee • ah) Land Company sent Daniel Boone to settle Kentucky. Boone did something that brought many settlers. Using axes, he and his men cleared a path through the Cumberland Gap. The trail they built from Virginia to central Kentucky was called the Wilderness Road.

Boone then built a town where his trail ended. It was named Boonesborough, after him.

The Revolutionary War began in 1775. Americans fought to free themselves from English rule. In Kentucky, many Indians sided with the English. They saw that the Americans were taking their lands. The

Ohio

Pennsylvania

Maryland

WILDERNESS ROAD (as it would run
through present-day
states)

Block House (in what was formerly Virginia)

Missouri

West Virginia

Virginia

Boonesborough

Kentucky

Cumberland
Gap

Indians attacked Boonesborough and Harrodsburg.
Daniel Boone and George Rogers Clark helped fight off
the Indians.

Daniel Boone had started out looking for a good place
to hunt. But what he had done in Kentucky had made
him very famous. He had helped the Americans win the
Revolutionary War. He had built one of Kentucky's first
towns. He had blazed the Wilderness Road.

In the 1770s and 1780s, many people took the trail to
Kentucky. Tough, strong people went there. Those who
wanted fancy houses and carriages knew that Kentucky
wasn't the place for them.

11

Once they got to Kentucky, families chopped down trees. They built log cabins. The cabins were patched with mud to keep out the cold. Windows were just cut-out squares covered with animal skins. The settlers hunted deer, bears, and other game. They also began to grow corn. Food was cooked over the fireplace in big pots.

It was very hard to send supplies over the mountains to Kentucky. So the settlers made what they needed. They made chairs and furniture out of logs. They used clay to make bowls. Women spun their own yarn. They then wove it into cloth. Berry juice, tree bark, and onion skins were used to dye their clothes pretty colors.

If you were a Kentucky child in the late 1700s you would have corn-shuck dolls and wooden toys. You would use soap made out of bear grease and lye. Your school would be a log cabin where children of all ages studied together. The nearest doctor might be hundreds of miles away. So if you got sick you might be given medicine made out of plants.

Where a number of people settled in one place, towns were built. Frankfort, Louisville, Stanford (STAN • furd), and Lexington (LEX • ing • tun) were just four of the towns founded by 1790. In 1790, the population of Kentucky was almost 75,000.

"Make Kentucky a state!" Kentuckians told the United States government. At this time, Kentucky was part of the state of Virginia. Then, on June 1, 1792, Kentucky became our 15th state. The next year Frankfort became the state's capital city. Kentucky was nicknamed the *Bluegrass State.* That was because of its grasses that have blue blossoms in the spring.

Kentucky men became famous for being good hunters. They had to be good. A missed shot could mean that their families wouldn't have food. This shooting skill came in handy during the War of 1812, which the United States fought against England. Kentucky men helped the United States win the war's last battle, at New Orleans. A song, "The Hunters of Kentucky," was written about the state's great fighters. The song exaggerated a bit. It said that the Kentucky fighters were half horse and half alligator!

The people of Kentucky knew how to have fun, too.
They held parties, called "frolics (FROLL • ickz)."
Fiddlers played while people danced. Horse racing also
became popular. Before there were racetracks,
Kentuckians raced horses right through the streets of
Louisville and other cities. One early Kentucky historian
joked that everyone he knew had a gun, a violin, and a
horse!

Thoroughbred horses are raised in Kentucky.

Many of the things that Kentucky is famous for today were developed in the early 1800s. It was found that Kentucky's Bluegrass Region was great for raising horses. The grass was good food. The water in the area had healthy minerals. Work horses as well as racehorses were bred. A kind of racehorse known as the *Thoroughbred* (THUR • oh • bred) was raised in large numbers in the Bluegrass Region.

During the 1800s whiskey became an important Kentucky product. A special kind of whiskey, called *bourbon* (BUR • bon), was first made in Kentucky. It was made from corn. Kentucky bourbon is now famous around the world.

16

Farmers found that Kentucky had the warm climate needed by the tobacco plant. Tobacco-growing became very important in the 1830s. Some rich tobacco farmers built large farms, called *plantations* (plan • TAY • shunz). Slaves did the work of growing the tobacco on the plantations. By the time the Civil War began, Kentucky was the leading tobacco-growing state.

Hemp was another big Kentucky farm crop before the Civil War. Hemp is a plant. At one time, a lot of hemp was used to make ropes for sailing ships. Slaves worked the hemp fields, too.

Tobacco (left) and corn (below) are still important crops.

During the 1850s people in the North and the South argued. Southerners felt that the United States government would soon end slavery. Southerners spoke of States' Rights. They felt that each state should decide for itself about slavery, taxes, and other matters.

The talking ended. Southerners formed their own country. They called it the Confederate (con • FED • er • it) States of America. The Confederate (Southern) states began to fight the Union (Northern) states in 1861. This was the start of the Civil War.

Kentucky is often called a Southern state. But if you look at a map you can see that Kentucky is really a border state. It lies between the North and the South.

Which side would Kentucky fight on? Some slave-owners wanted Kentucky to leave the Union and fight for the South. Others wanted the state to fight for the North. Kentucky did stay in the Union. But Kentuckians fought on both sides. About 75,000 Kentuckians fought for the North. About 35,000 fought for the South.

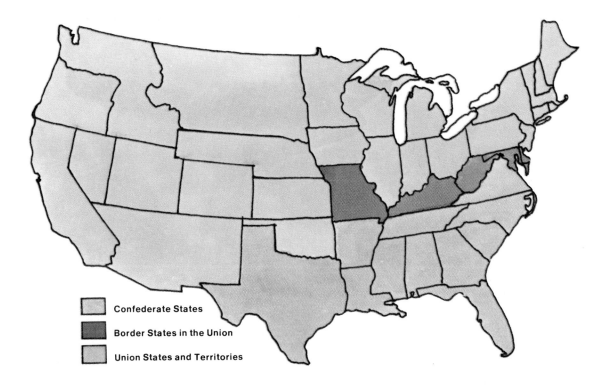

	Confederate States
	Border States in the Union
	Union States and Territories

The Civil War was the bloodiest war in our country's history. It was especially heartbreaking in Kentucky. Members of a family sometimes found themselves shooting at each other on battlefields.

Kentucky also produced the two men who led the North and the South during the Civil War. Amazingly, they were born within 100 miles of each other. They were born less than a year apart.

Abraham Lincoln was born on February 12, 1809, in a log cabin near Hodgenville, Kentucky. Lincoln became the 16th president of the United States and led the North during the Civil War.

Jefferson Davis was born on June 3, 1808, where the town of Fairview now stands. He became the president of the Confederacy and led the South during the Civil War.

Top right: Cannon and Confederate Monument at Perryville Battlefield
Bottom right: Abraham Lincoln's boyhood home at Knob Creek
Below: Jefferson Davis

There were some big battles inside Kentucky. In January of 1862 the North won an important battle at Mill Springs. That August, the South won a battle at Richmond. The biggest Civil War battle in Kentucky was at Perryville. It was fought on October 8, 1862. About 6,500 men were killed or wounded. Neither side won the Battle of Perryville. But afterwards the Southern army had to retreat to Tennessee.

The North had more soldiers. It had more supplies. In 1865 the North won the Civil War.

After the Civil War, much of the old way of life in Kentucky was ended. The slaves were free. Tobacco-growers now had to pay people to work on the farms. Tobacco was still a big crop. But hemp was no longer important. As steamships replaced sailing ships, the hemp was no longer needed.

Do you remember how people once raced horses through the streets of Louisville? In 1875 a racetrack was opened in Louisville. It was called Churchill (CHER • chill) Downs. The first year it opened, a race called the Kentucky Derby was held there. This yearly event became the most famous horse race in the United States.

In the late 1800s many railroads were built in Kentucky. Railroads meant a lot to the state. Trains could now carry lumber, coal, and other products out of Kentucky.

Coal became a main Kentucky product. Coal was used to heat buildings. It was used to run steamships, trains, and machines. It was used in the making of steel.

The men who mined the coal had hard, dangerous jobs. Accidents in the mines killed some men. Coal dust gave many lung diseases. Miners also worked long hours underground for low pay.

Coal miner at work

Miners joined a *union*. This was a group of people working together to improve mining conditions. Sometimes there were fights between the miners' union and mine owners. In the 1930s there were so many battles in Harlan County that it was called "Bloody Harlan." Today, mining is still hard work. But laws have been passed to give miners more pay and safer working conditions.

Today, Kentucky is the number one coal-mining state in the United States. The Bluegrass State is also the leading state for making whiskey. And it is a top state for growing tobacco.

Powell Valley, Cumberland Gap

You have learned about some of Kentucky's history. Now it is time for a trip—in words and pictures—through the Bluegrass State.

Kentucky is much longer in east to west distance than it is from north to south. Except for the fairly straight southern border, Kentucky is shaped much like a tobacco leaf. Seven states border Kentucky. They are Indiana, Ohio, West Virginia, Virginia, Tennessee, Missouri, and Illinois.

Pretend you are in an airplane high above Kentucky. From the air, the state is bright with green and blue colors. Rivers—such as the Ohio, the Green, and the Kentucky—can be seen. In eastern Kentucky you see the Appalachian Mountains. A lot of coal mining is done there. In the central part of Kentucky you see the Bluegrass Region. This is a big farming and horse-raising area. Much of the hilly western part of the state is called the Western Coal Field. You probably can tell that a lot of coal is mined there, too!

Your airplane is landing in a city in northern Kentucky. This is Louisville. The city lies on the Ohio River.

Louisville at night

This fountain in a modern plaza attracts waders.

Long ago, Shawnee and Cherokee Indians hunted here.
During the Revolutionary War, George Rogers Clark led
some soldiers and families into this area. They built a
settlement. Clark named it *Louisville* to thank the
French King Louis XVI for helping us win the
Revolutionary War. Today, Louisville is Kentucky's
biggest city.

You'll see many kinds of people in Louisville. About a
fourth of the city's people are black. There are also
people of German, Irish, Italian, and many other ethnic
backgrounds.

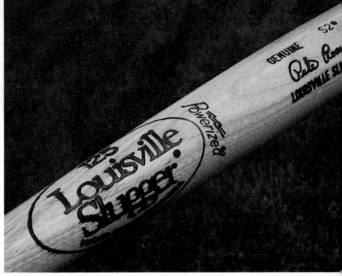

Far left: Tobacco leaves are hung to dry
Left: Worker on whiskey assembly line
Above: Louisville Slugger baseball bat

The people of Louisville make many products. Louisville is one of the world's leading cities for making cigarettes and other tobacco products. It's also a big whiskey-making city. Paint, lumber, electrical appliances, and chemicals are four other Louisville products. Baseball bats, called "Louisville Sluggers," are made near the city. Louisville also has a special printing house. It is the American Printing House for the Blind. Books are printed there in *braille*. Blind people can read them by touch.

Once, most Louisville products left the city by boat on the Ohio River. Today, boats as well as airplanes, trucks, and trains take Louisville products to other cities.

Above: Giraffe at Louisville Zoo
Right: Portrait of George Rogers Clark
Far right: Locust Grove

There are many interesting places to visit in
Louisville. At the Museum of Natural History and
Science you can learn about space travel and caves. At
the Kentucky Railway Museum you can see old trains.
You'll enjoy Locust Grove. It was the last home of
George Rogers Clark. Clark did many other things
besides found Louisville. During the Revolutionary War,
he led American soldiers to big wins against the English
in Illinois and Indiana. Clark couldn't get money from
the government to pay his men. So he paid them with his
own money! George Rogers Clark lived the last nine
years of his life here at Locust Grove.

Louisville is world-famous for horse racing. The Kentucky Derby is held at Churchill Downs on the first Saturday in May. This race is called the "Run for the Roses" because the winning horse receives a blanket of roses around its neck. The owner of the winning horse gets more than roses! In 1980, the winner received over $250,000.

Visit the Zachary Taylor National Cemetery near Louisville. Back in 1785, a baby named Zachary Taylor moved to Kentucky with his family. Zachary Taylor became a soldier. Later, he became the 12th President of the United States.

Far left: Museum of Natural History and Science
Left: Portrait of Zachary Taylor
Below: Kentucky Derby, Churchill Downs

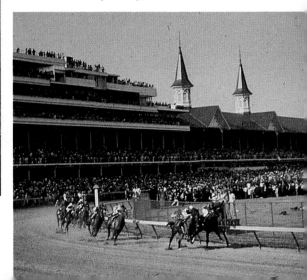

Above: Covington
Right: Gold bars in vault at Fort Knox

About 30 miles south of Louisville you will come to
Fort Knox. It is an army post. The U.S. Treasury
Department stores gold at Fort Knox, in underground
vaults. About six *billion* dollars worth of gold is kept
there. You'll hear Fort Knox mentioned a lot when
people talk of places that have a lot of money.

From Fort Knox, head northeast to Covington (CUV •
ing • tun). The city lies in far northern Kentucky. It is on
the Ohio River. A lot of metal products are made in
Covington. When boats were a main way of traveling
through Kentucky, many cities besides Covington were
built on the Ohio River. Owensboro (OH • wenz • burro)
and Paducah (pah • DOO • cah) are two of those cities.

Above: State Capitol, Frankfort
Left: Old Capitol, now the Kentucky Historical Society

Southwest of Covington you will come to Frankfort.
Frankfort was founded in 1786. When Kentucky became
a state in 1792, many cities asked to be the state capital.
Kentucky lawmakers picked Frankfort. It has been the
capital of the Bluegrass State for almost 200 years.

Do you see that building with the big dome? That is
Kentucky's State Capitol building. Lawmakers from all
across Kentucky meet here. You can watch them
working on laws for the Bluegrass State.

Visit the Old Capitol in Frankfort. Kentucky
lawmakers met here until 1910. The Kentucky Historical
Society now makes its home here.

Liberty Hall

You'll also enjoy Frankfort's "Corner of Celebrities (seh • LEB • rih • teez)." It's a section of the city that has many fancy houses. Supreme Court judges, United States senators, and famous generals have lived here.

Because Frankfort is in Kentucky's Bluegrass Region, it is sometimes called the *Bluegrass Capital*. The city of Lexington is in the heart of the Bluegrass Region. You'll see lots of horse farms near Lexington. You can visit many of them.

Many of Kentucky's horses are raised for racing. Kentuckians are proud that horses from their state have won the Kentucky Derby most of the time.

Man o' War statue

If you'd like to learn about horses, visit the Kentucky Horse Park, just north of Lexington. There you can learn how horses have changed over millions of years. You can learn about the many breeds of horses. You'll see a statue of Man o' War at the Kentucky Horse Park. He was one of the greatest racehorses of all time. A man named Isaac Murphy (EYE • zack MER • fee) is buried near the Man o' War statue. Murphy was a great black jockey of the late 1800s. He won the Kentucky Derby three times.

Head into Lexington. The town was founded in 1779. Today, Lexington is Kentucky's second biggest city.

A lot of Kentucky horses are bought and sold in Lexington. Tobacco farmers in the area send their crops to Lexington. The tobacco is bought by tobacco companies.

Above: Ashland, home of Henry Clay
Right: Mary Todd Lincoln House

The first college built west of the Allegheny (al • ih •
GAIN • ee) Mountains is in Lexington. It is called
Transylvania University, and it was founded in 1780. The
University of Kentucky is also in Lexington.

You'll enjoy the Mary Todd Lincoln House in
Lexington. Mary Todd spent her girlhood here. She later
became the wife of President Abraham Lincoln.

A man who wanted to be president also lived in
Lexington. His name was Henry Clay. You can visit his
house, called "Ashland." Clay became a United States
senator when he was only 29 years old. He tried to help
our country avoid the Civil War. Henry Clay ran for

Loading coal cars

president three times—but lost each time. Clay felt so strongly about his beliefs that he once said: "I had rather be right than be President."

From Lexington, head into the Appalachian Mountains of eastern Kentucky. You'll see a lot of coal mines. The coal in Kentucky is *bituminous* (by • TOO • mih • nus). That means that it's soft coal.

There are many small towns around the coal mines in eastern Kentucky. Not everyone in eastern Kentucky mines coal, however. You'll find people who live on small farms.

Some mountain people have kept their old customs. They sing songs that are hundreds of years old. Some still make their own clothes, chairs, musical instruments, and housewares.

Daniel Boone National Forest is in eastern Kentucky. In all, about half the state is covered by forests. You'll see many animals in the woods. There are thought to be more deer in Kentucky now than there were in Daniel Boone's time. Foxes, bobcats, raccoons, and beavers can also be seen. Eagles and hawks are just two of the birds you might spot.

From Daniel Boone National Forest, head west to see some places near the middle of the state. Visit Fort Boonesborough. It has been rebuilt to look as it did in the 1770s, when Daniel Boone founded it.

Right: Daniel Boone National Forest
Below: Federal Hall

Kentucky's state song is "My Old Kentucky Home." It was written by Stephen Foster. West of Fort Boonesborough visit the house called Federal Hill, near Bardstown. A visit to this house gave Stephen Foster the idea for "My Old Kentucky Home."

Not far from this house go to the Abraham Lincoln Birthplace National Historic Site, near Hodgenville. There you can see the log cabin thought to be the birthplace of our 16th president. When Abe was very little, his family moved to a farm on Knob Creek, a few miles away. Abe went to a "blab school." That was a school where all the children said their lessons at the same time. It must have been noisy! But that way the teacher knew they were all doing the lesson. Abe Lincoln didn't stay long in Kentucky. When he was just seven years old, his family moved to Indiana.

Mammoth Cave, Cave City, Kentucky

Kentucky has thousands of caves. Southwest of Abraham Lincoln's birthplace you will come to Mammoth Cave. Water and chemicals carved it out over millions of years. Mammoth Cave is the longest cave system in the world. It has over 200 miles of underground passages.

You'll see many weird-shaped rocks in Mammoth Cave. The cave also has lakes, waterfalls, and underground rivers. Many animals live in the cave. There are bats and spiders. Strange fish that don't have eyes live in the cave's Echo (ECKOH) River. They are called blindfish. Eyes wouldn't do them any good. It's dark in there!

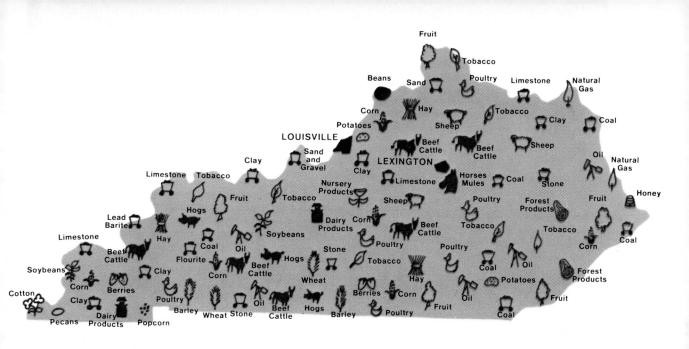

After seeing Mammoth Cave, go on to visit western Kentucky. You'll see many tobacco farms in western Kentucky—and in many other areas of the state. Tobacco is the state's main crop. But many other crops are grown in the Bluegrass State. You'll see fields of corn and soybeans. Barley, hay, oats, popcorn, and peaches are also grown. Some Kentucky farmers raise milk cows. Others raise beef cattle. Chickens, hogs, and sheep are some of the other livestock raised in Kentucky.

Some farmers in southwestern Kentucky send farm products to the city of Bowling Green. Tobacco is bought and sold there. Milk is packaged there. Bowling Green is also the home of Western Kentucky University.

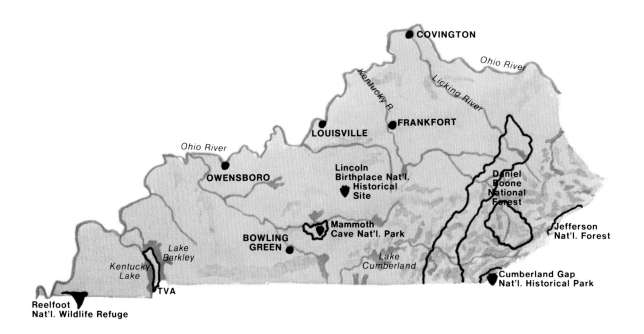

Finish your Kentucky trip by visiting the Ancient Buried City. It is in far western Kentucky, near Wickliffe (WHY • cliff). Indians lived in this village 1,000 years ago. Their bones have been found in a big burial mound. Their homes and temples have been uncovered here, too.

Places can't tell the whole story of Kentucky. Many interesting people have lived in the Bluegrass State.

John C. Breckinridge (BRECK • en • ridge) (1821-1875) was born near Lexington. From 1857 to 1861 he served as the 14th vice-president of the United States. But when the Civil War began, Breckinridge sided with the

South. He fought in a number of battles as a Confederate general. After the Civil War, Breckinridge helped develop railroads in his home state. Richard M. Johnson, Adlai E. Stevenson, and Alben W. Barkley were three other vice-presidents born in Kentucky.

Daniel Carter Beard (1850-1941) was born in Cincinnati, Ohio. But he grew up just across the Ohio River in Covington, Kentucky. Beard formed a group called the "Sons of Daniel Boone." Later this group became the Boy Scouts of America.

Whitney M. Young, Jr., (1921-1971) was a black leader born in Lincoln Ridge, Kentucky. He became the head of the Urban League. Young helped many blacks get jobs. He founded Head Start centers, which get children off to a good start in school. Whitney M. Young, Jr., also wrote the book *To Be Equal.*

Loretta Lynn was born in the coal-mining village of Butcher Hollow in eastern Kentucky. She had four children by the time she was 18, and was a grandmother at 27. Loretta Lynn liked to sing. Her children enjoyed her songs—and so did many other people. After years of work, she became one of the biggest stars of country music. You may have heard Loretta Lynn sing. The film, *Coal Miner's Daughter,* tells the story of her life.

One of the greatest sports figures of all time was born in Louisville in 1942. His name is Muhammad Ali (moo • HAH • med ah • LEE). Ali won a gold medal in boxing at the 1960 Olympics. When he became a pro, Ali predicted the round that he'd win his fights. Often, he was right. Ali is the only boxer ever to have won the heavyweight crown three separate times.

Steve Cauthen was born in Covington, Kentucky, in 1960. He rode ponies when he was just two years old. Cauthen learned to ride well, and he never grew very big. Steve Cauthen became a great jockey. He won the Kentucky Derby when he was just 18 years old.

Pinnacles Overlook, Cumberland Gap

Home to Daniel Boone . . . Abraham Lincoln . . . Jefferson Davis . . . Loretta Lynn . . . and Thoroughbred horses.

The leading coal-mining state . . . the leading whiskey-making state . . . and a leader in growing tobacco.

A land where you can see the Bluegrass country . . . Mammoth Cave . . . and lovely mountains.

This is one of the prettiest places on Earth— Kentucky!

Facts About KENTUCKY

Area—40,395 square miles

Greatest Distance North to South—175 miles

Greatest Distance East to West—350 miles

Border States—Indiana, Ohio, West Virginia, Virginia, Tennessee, Missouri, and Illinois

Highest Point—4,145 feet above sea level (Black Mountain)

Lowest Point—257 feet above sea level (along the Mississippi River)

Hottest Recorded Temperature—114° (at Greensburg, on July 28, 1930)

Coldest Recorded Temperature—Minus 34° (at Cynthiana, on January 28, 1963)

Statehood—Our 15th state, on June 1, 1792

Origin of Name—*Kentucky* comes from an Indian word; some think it means the *Land of Tomorrow,* while others say it means the *Dark and Bloody Ground* or the *Meadowland*

Capital—Frankfort (1793)

Previous Capital—Lexington

Counties—120

U.S. Senators—2

U.S. Representatives—7

State Senators—38

State Representatives—100

State Song—"My Old Kentucky Home," by Stephen Collins Foster

State Motto—*United We Stand, Divided We Fall*

Nickname—The Bluegrass State

State Seal—Adopted in 1792, the year of statehood

State Flag—Adopted in 1918

State Flower—Goldenrod

State Bird—Kentucky cardinal

State Wild Animal—Gray squirrel

State Fish—Kentucky bass (also called the spotted bass)

State Tree—Kentucky coffeetree

44

Some Rivers—Ohio, Kentucky, Mississippi, Green, Licking, Barren, Big Sandy, Tradewater

Some Lakes—Kentucky Lake, Rough River Lake, Nolin Lake, Barren River Lake, Green River Lake, Dale Hollow Lake, Lake Cumberland

Highest Waterfall—Cumberland Falls

National Parklands—Mammoth Cave National Park
Abraham Lincoln Birthplace National Historic Site
Cumberland Gap National Historical Park

Wildlife—Deer, foxes, bobcats, raccoons, beavers, rabbits, minks, muskrats, opossums, woodchucks, bats, many kinds of snakes and turtles, cardinals, woodpeckers, herons, eagles, hawks, grouse, quail, many other kinds of birds

Fishing—Bass, trout, bluegill, crappie, catfish, walleye, carp

Farm Products—Tobacco, corn, soybeans, wheat, hay, rye, oats, popcorn, peaches, apples, race horses, beef cattle, milk cows, chickens, eggs, hogs, sheep

Mining—Coal, oil, natural gas, fluorite, clays

Manufacturing Products—Machinery, whiskey, meat products and other foods, electrical appliances, chemicals, tobacco products, clothes, metals

Population—3,458,000 (1977 estimate)

Major Cities—Louisville   310,000 (all 1979 estimates)
Lexington   193,200
Owensboro   50,700
Covington   43,900
Bowling Green 38,800
Paducah   32,800

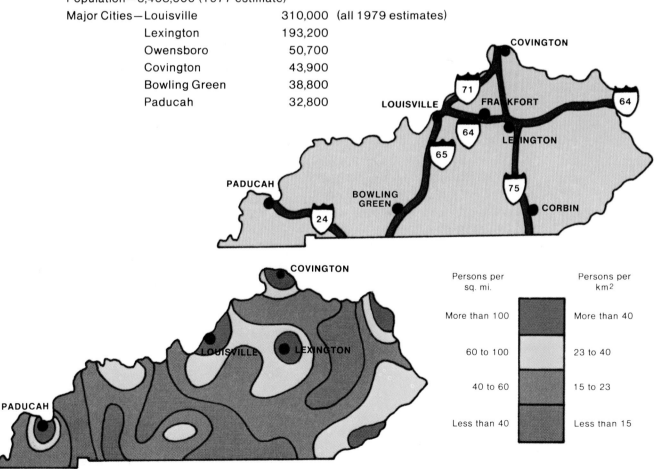

Persons per sq. mi.	Persons per km2
More than 100	More than 40
60 to 100	23 to 40
40 to 60	15 to 23
Less than 40	Less than 15

Kentucky History

It is thought that Indians came to Kentucky at least 15,000 years ago.

1750—Dr. Thomas Walker passes through Cumberland Gap and then explores Kentucky

1767—Daniel Boone first comes to Kentucky

1769—Boone returns, and spends two years on a "long hunt"

1774—James Harrod founds Harrodsburg, the first permanent non-Indian settlement in Kentucky

1775—Daniel Boone blazes Wilderness Road and then founds Boonesborough

1775-1783—During the Revolutionary War, Daniel Boone and George Rogers Clark help defend Kentucky against Indian attacks

1776—Kentucky is made a county of Virginia

1778—George Rogers Clark helps to found Louisville

1779—Lexington is permanently settled

1780—Transylvania University, the first college west of the Allegheny Mountains, is founded

1786—Frankfort is founded

1790—Population of Kentucky nears 75,000

1792—On June 1, Kentucky becomes our 15th state; Lexington is the capital

1793—Frankfort becomes the capital

1808—On June 3, Jefferson Davis is born at what is now Fairview

1809—On February 12, Abraham Lincoln is born near Hodgenville

1815—Kentuckians help win the Battle of New Orleans, the last battle of the War of 1812; in this same year the first steamboat to go up the Mississippi and Ohio rivers, the *Enterprise,* travels from New Orleans to Louisville

1818—A deal with the Indians, called the "Jackson Purchase," adds more land to western Kentucky

1830s—Tobacco farming becomes important

1861—Civil War begins; Kentucky officially is on the Union side, but Kentucky men fight on both the Union and Confederate sides

1862—On January 19, Union soldiers win a battle at Mill Springs; in August the Confederates win a battle at Richmond; on October 8 the Battle of Perryville is fought, with about 6,500 men killed or wounded

1865—The North wins the Civil War; in this same year the University of Kentucky is founded

1875—Kentucky Derby horse race is first run

1891—Present state constitution is adopted

1900—Population of the Bluegrass State is 2,147,174; in this same year Governor William Goebel is shot and killed

1904-1909—During the "Black Patch War," tobacco farmers in western Kentucky fight tobacco companies

1909—State Capitol building is completed

1917-1918—After the United States enters World War I, 75,043 Kentuckians are in uniform

1930's—During the Great Depression, Kentucky farmers lose farms and coal miners lose jobs

1936—The United States Treasury Department creates a gold vault at Fort Knox

1937—Big flood hits state

1941—Mammoth Cave National Park is created

1941-1945—After the United States enters World War II, 323,798 Kentucky men and women are in uniform

1955—The voting age in the Bluegrass State is lowered to 18

1966—State lawmakers pass a Civil Rights Act

1968—State lawmakers pass a Fair Housing Act

1970—Population of the state reaches 3,219,311

1972—First tax on coal production is passed by state lawmakers

INDEX

About the Author:

Dennis Fradin attended Northwestern University on a creative writing scholarship and graduated in 1967. While still at Northwestern, he published his first stories in *Ingenue* magazine and also won a prize in *Seventeen's* short story competition. A prolific writer, Dennis Fradin has been regularly publishing stories in such diverse places as *The Saturday Evening Post, Scholastic, National Humane Review, Midwest,* and *The Teaching Paper.* He has also scripted several educational films. Since 1970 he has taught second grade reading in a Chicago school—a rewarding job, which, the author says, "provides a captive audience on whom I test my children's stories." Married and the father of three children, Dennis Fradin spends his free time with his family or playing a myriad of sports and games with his childhood chums.

About the Artists:

Len Meents studied painting and drawing at Southern Illinois University and after graduation in 1969 he moved to Chicago. Mr. Meents works full time as a painter and illustrator. He and his wife and child currently make their home in LaGrange, Illinois.

Richard Wahl, graduate of the Art Center College of Design in Los Angeles, has illustrated a number of magazine articles and booklets. He is a skilled artist and photographer who advocates realistic interpretations of his subjects. He lives with his wife and two sons in Libertyville, Illinois.